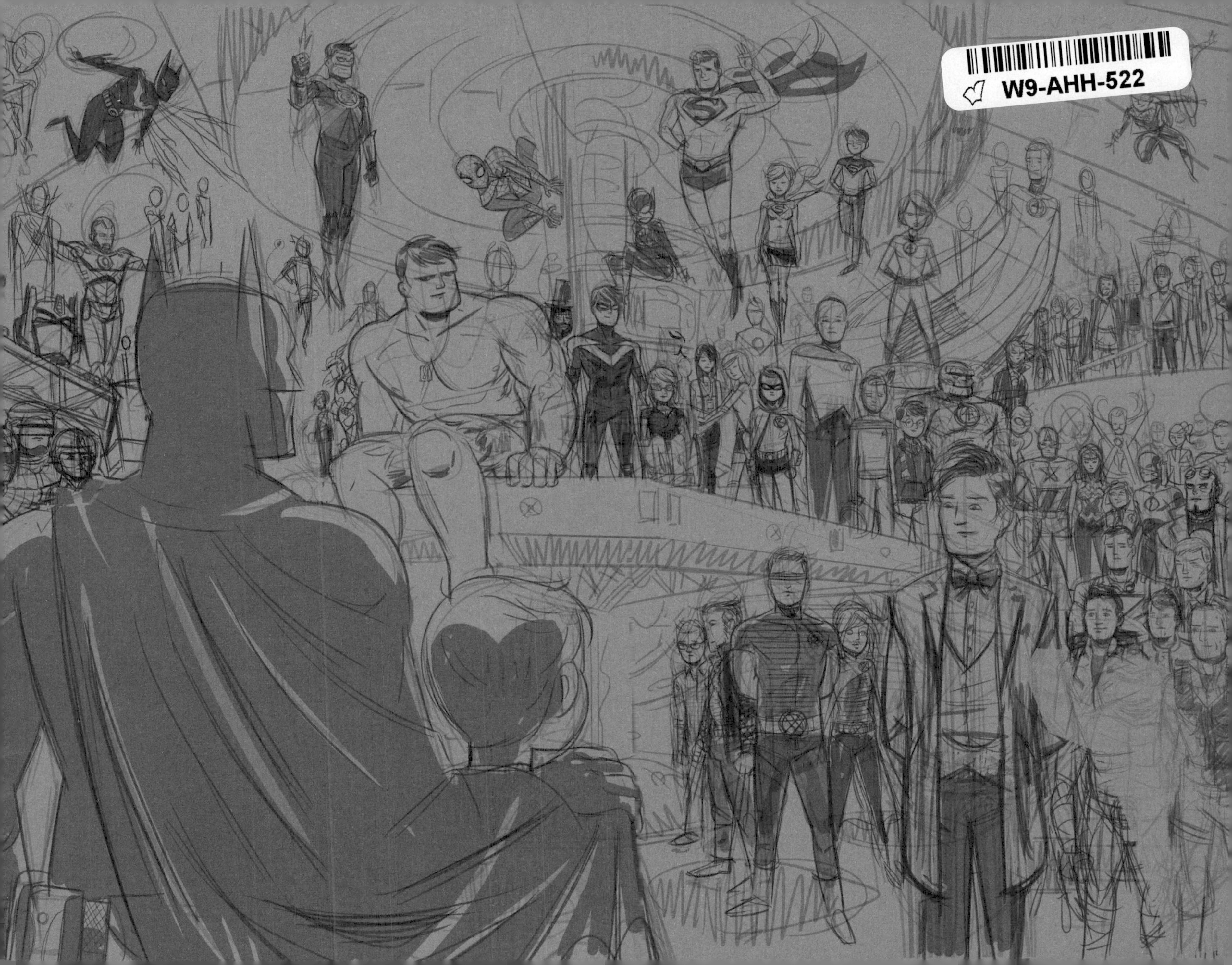

Something TERRIBLE

Story & Art by Dean Trippe

Logo Design by Hannah Nance Partlow

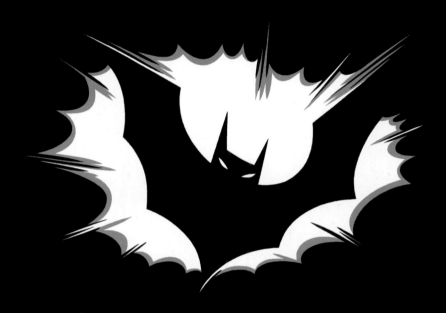

NOTE: This book is an autobiographical fan comic and is not intended for children.

FOREWORD

I've always known Dean's work to be lovingly and firmly entrenched in the superhero genre. Celebrating it, challenging it, and finding the heart in it.

His approach has always seemed, to me, welcoming, whether running a site for superhero costume redesigns, open to anyone who'd like to try their hand, or a writing a YA pitch for girls that respects its intended audience as new fans, or creating a new series of his own like the light-hearted and hopeful *Butterfly*.

Historically, comics have been unceremoniously lumped together as one genre, which they aren't. And in the comics community, we sometimes draw our own lines. I come from a different comics neighbourhood, one not of superheroes, but of gag jokes. My trade is in funny, rather than fantasy.

Even so, I've soaked up the world of superheroes; they loom so large in comics culture, they're almost bound to draw you in. But I look with the most interest even further downfield, to the real world stories told in autobiographical comics. I think most of us wish we had the guts to lay aside all the funny and fantasy and dig into something real.

I guess that's my way of saying that I did not expect *Something Terrible*. I didn't think this sort of autobiography was in Dean's wheelhouse. But of course, the genre lines we draw are arbitrary. When you're a good storyteller, storytelling is your wheelhouse, period.

Something Terrible is a story that knocked me clear out.

At their best, superhero comics show us our world through a lens that makes us think harder on what we value, what we fight for, what we can be as people, what choices we could make, and what choices we have. And at their best, autobiographical comics can be unflinching, honest and unafraid to let the ugly truths out. Because odds are, our secrets are more relatable than we'd expect. Something Terrible does all of these things, with a story of the real world none of us wish we had to see— though far too many have—through a new lens fashioned of fact and fantasy.

I always thought that the welcoming approach of Dean's superhero work gave it an intentional aura of relative innocence, working in a genre that too often fights to be seen as especially brutal. I see now that he does fight for innocence, and he believes in the super power of heroes. We need our heroes.

Dean Trippe is one of mine.

Kate Beaton
Hark! A Vagrant

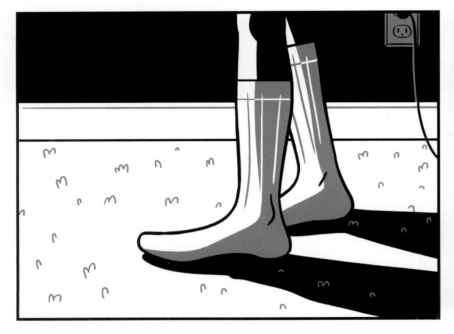

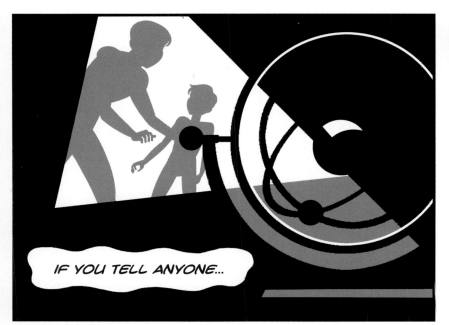

IF YOU TELL ANYONE...

...I'LL KILL YOUR FAMILY.

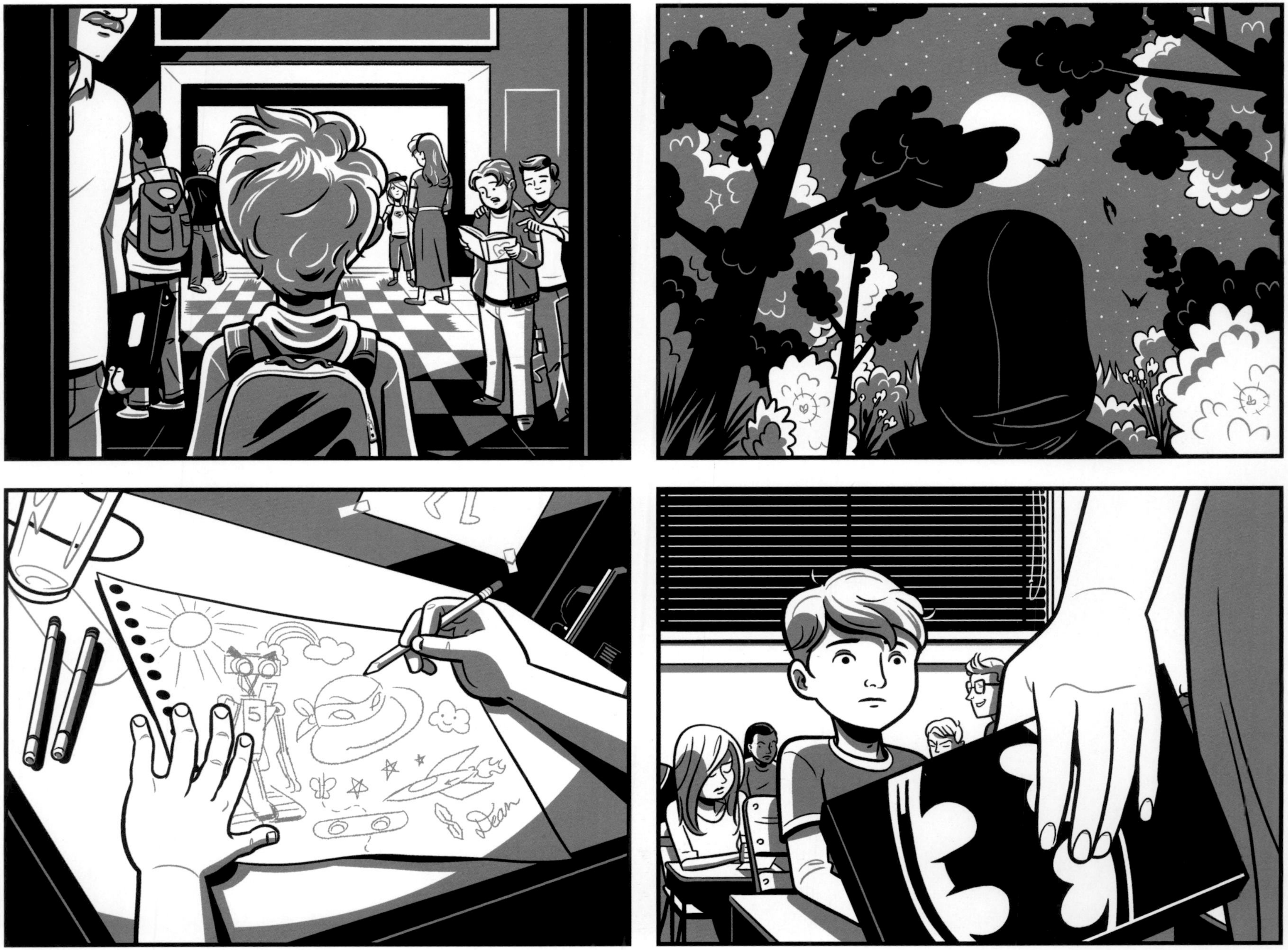
5
Dean

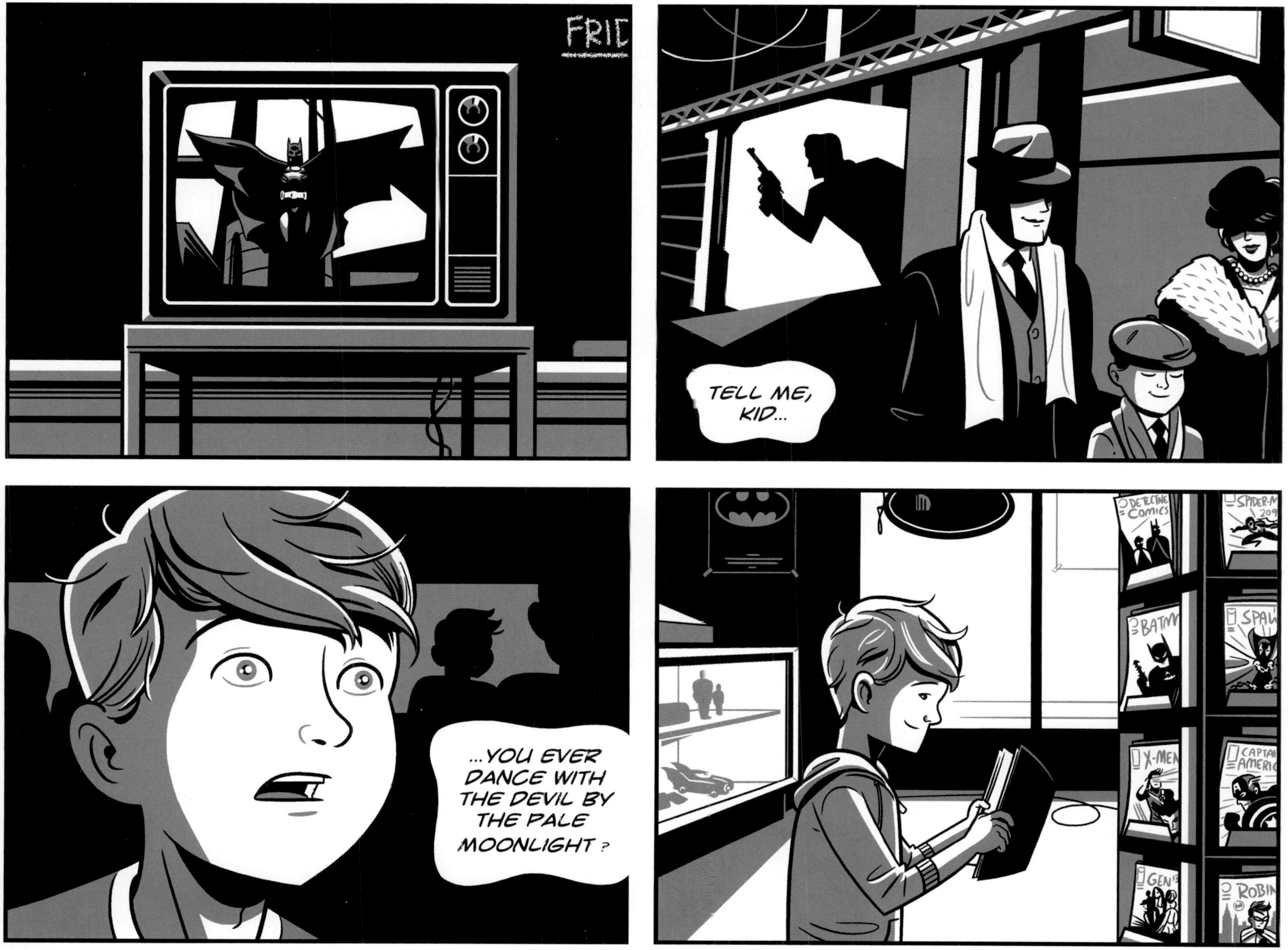
FRID
TELL ME, KID...
...YOU EVER DANCE WITH THE DEVIL BY THE PALE MOONLIGHT?
DETECTIVE COMICS
X-MEN
ROBIN

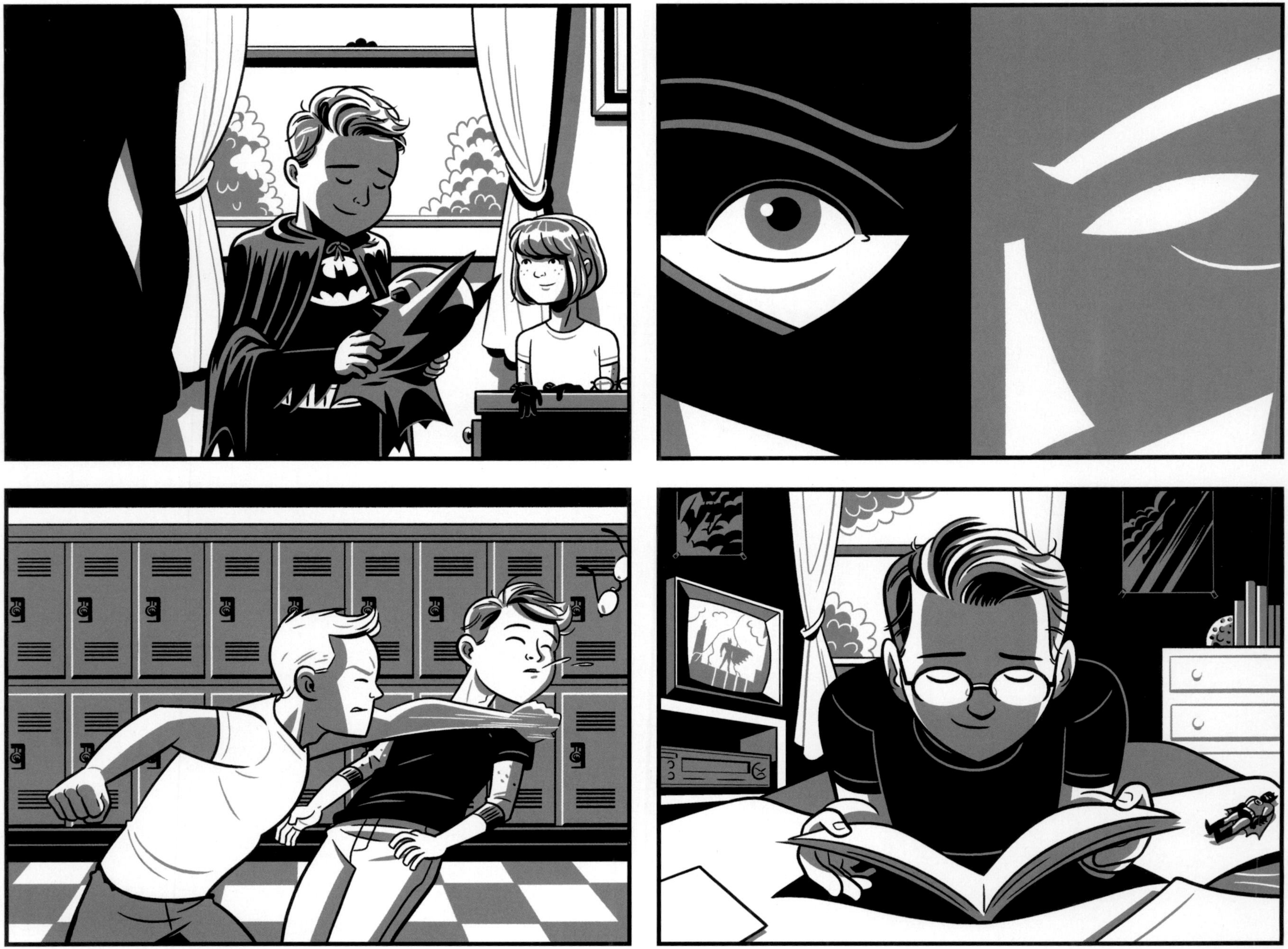

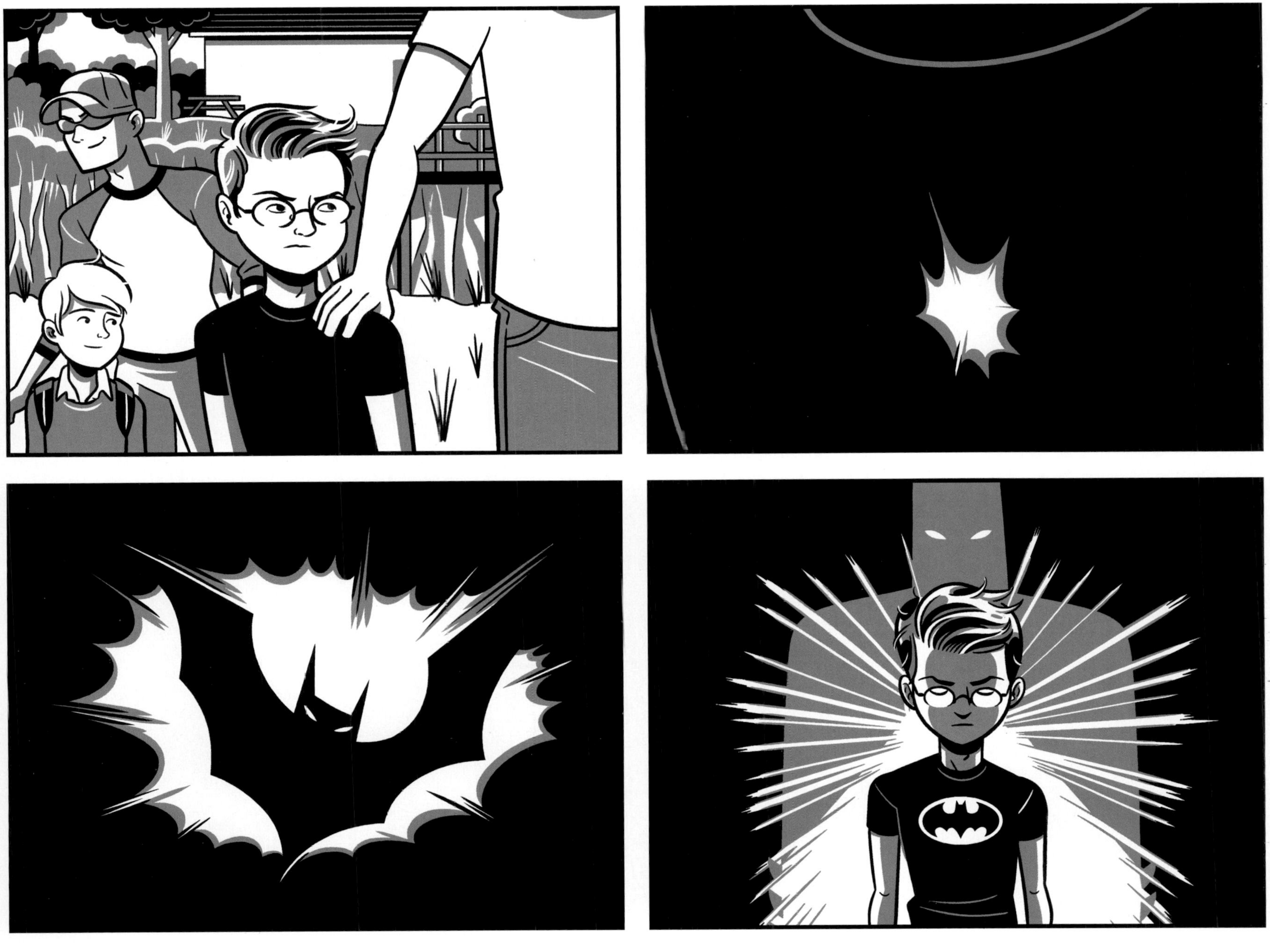

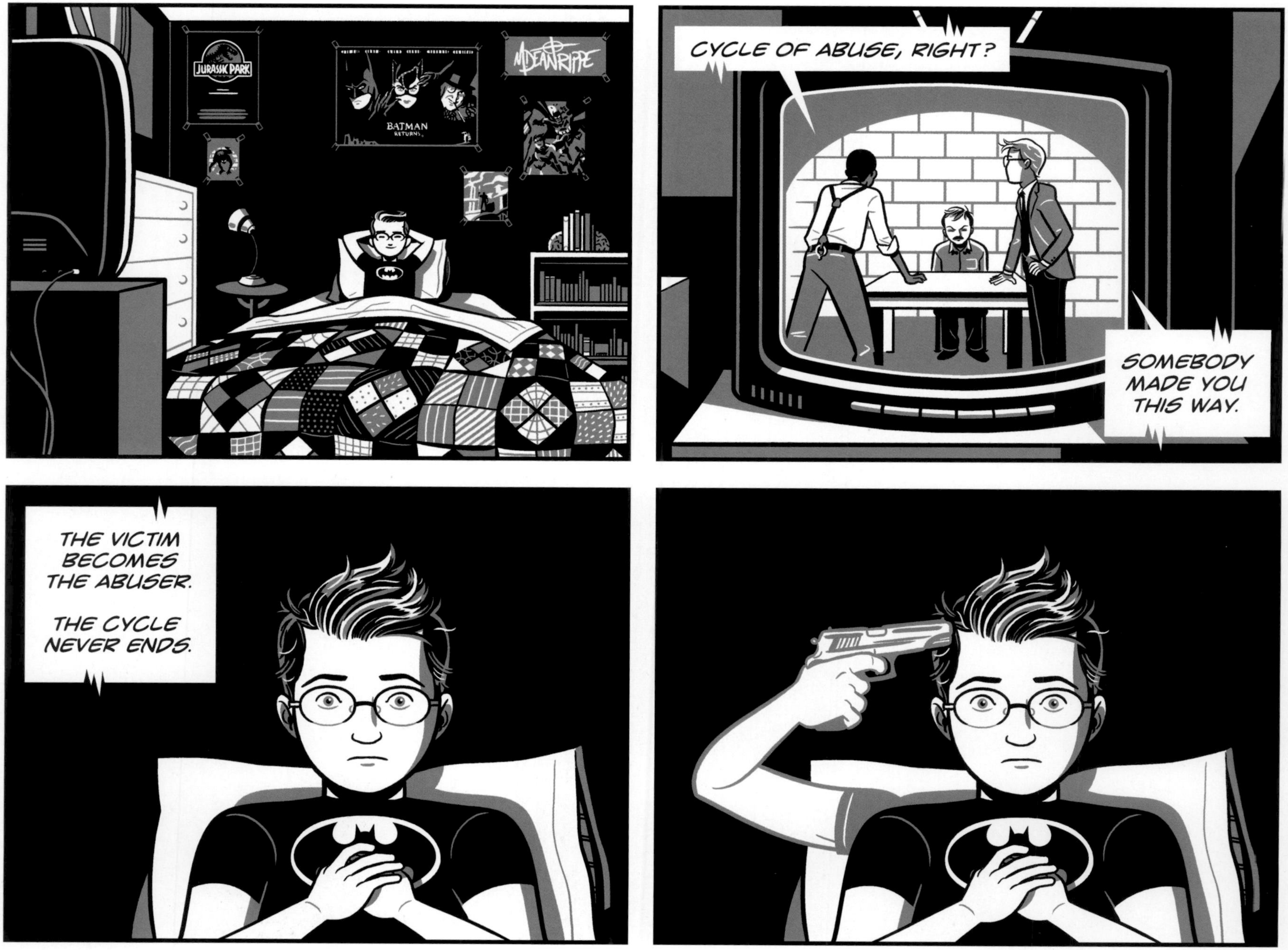
JURASSIC PARK
BATMAN RETURNS
CYCLE OF ABUSE, RIGHT?
SOMEBODY MADE YOU THIS WAY.
THE VICTIM BECOMES THE ABUSER.
THE CYCLE NEVER ENDS.

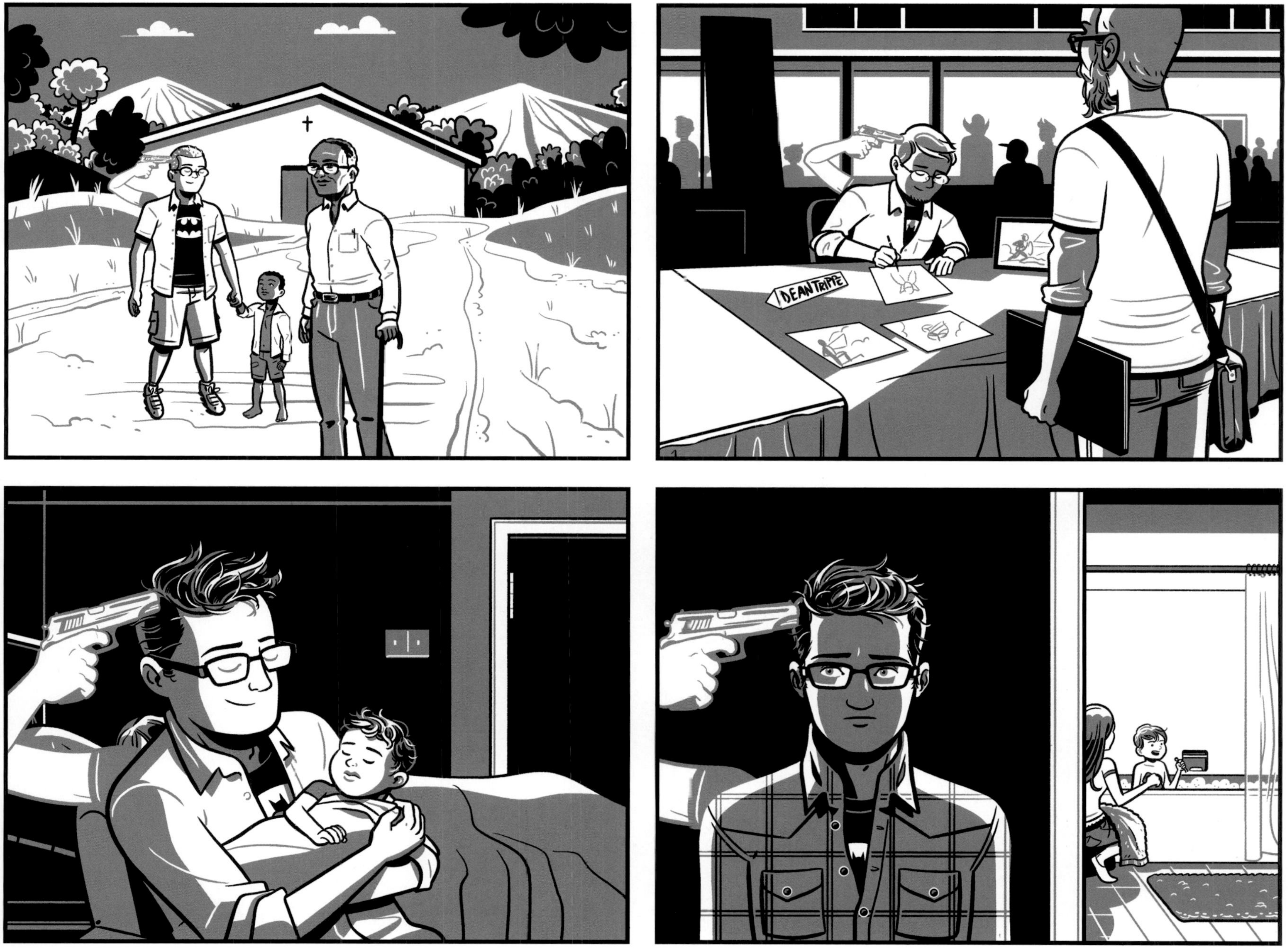
DEAN TRIPPE

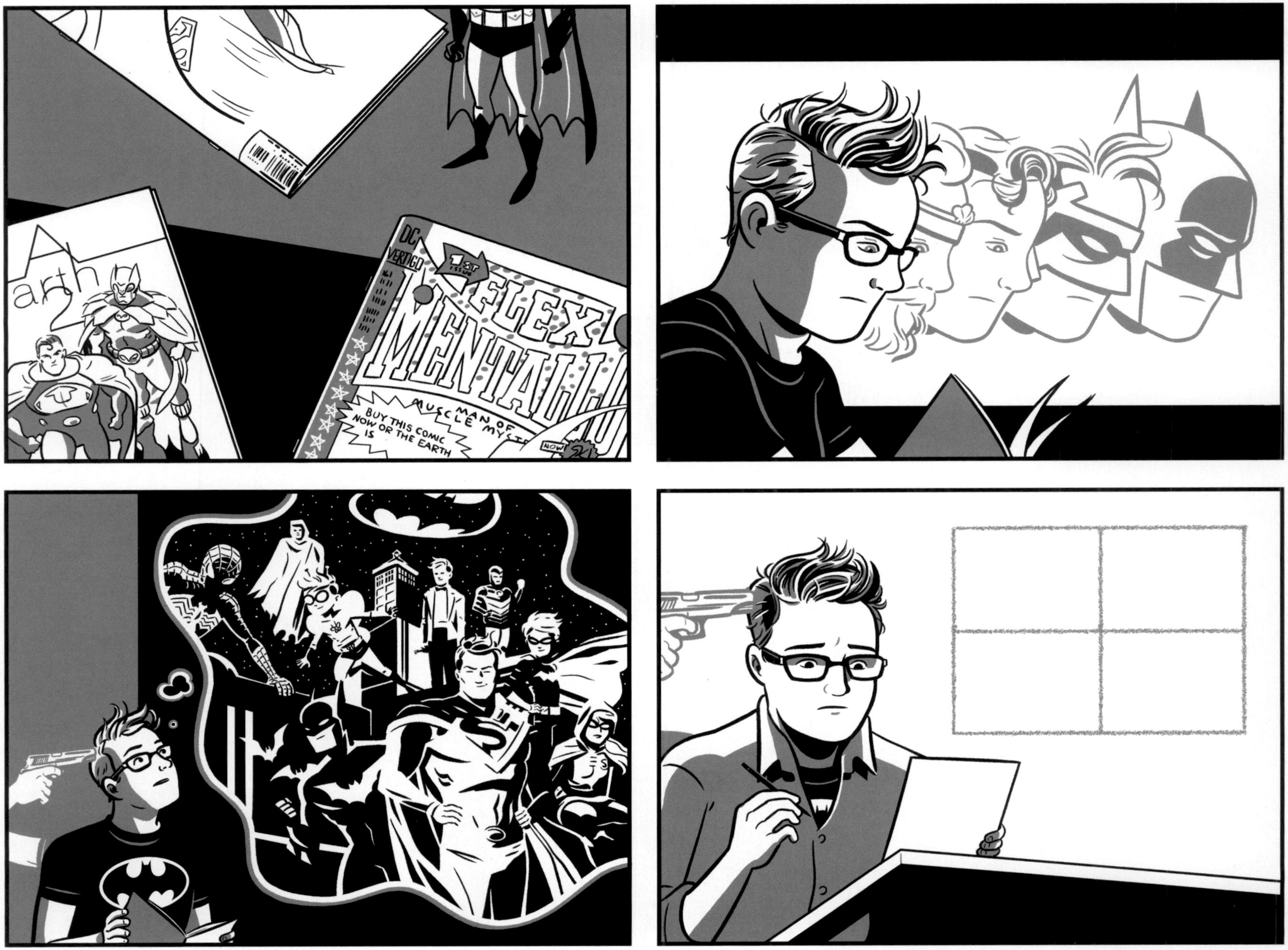
DC
VERTIGO
1ST
FLEX
MAN OF
BUY THIS COMIC
NOW OR THE EARTH
IS
NOW

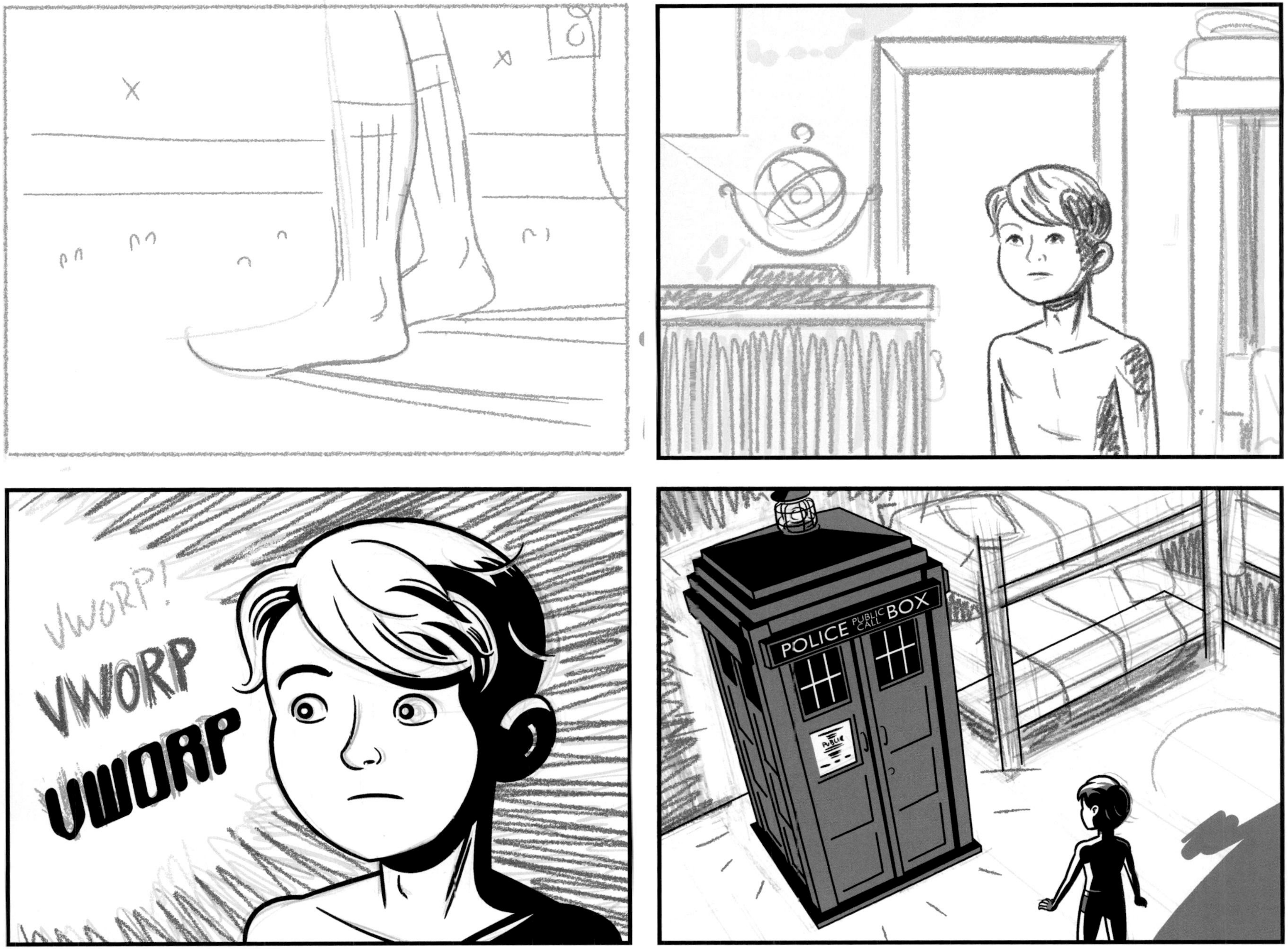
VWORP!
VWORP
VWORP
POLICE PUBLIC CALL BOX

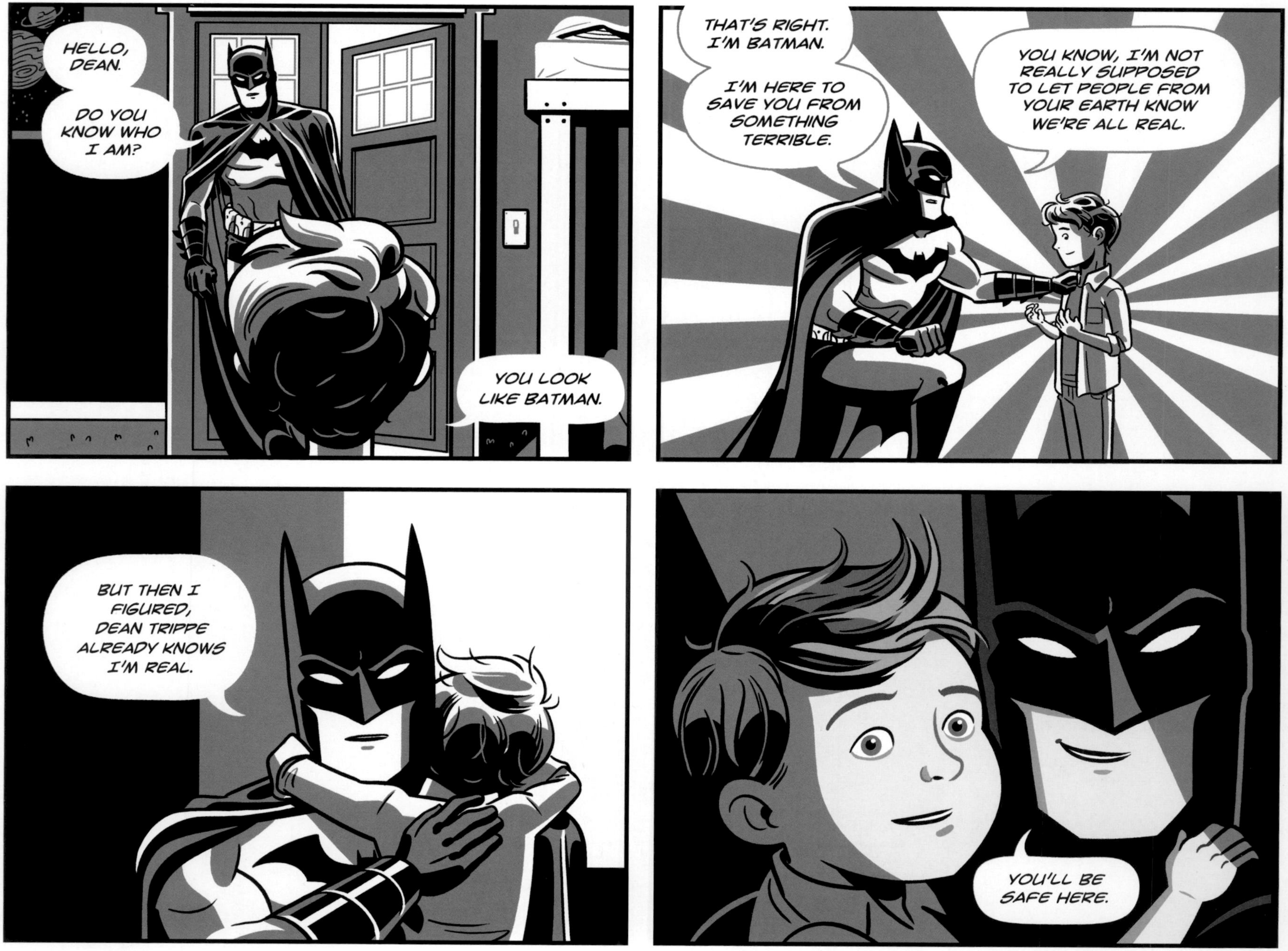
HELLO, DEAN.
DO YOU KNOW WHO I AM?
YOU LOOK LIKE BATMAN.
THAT'S RIGHT. I'M BATMAN.
I'M HERE TO SAVE YOU FROM SOMETHING TERRIBLE.
YOU KNOW, I'M NOT REALLY SUPPOSED TO LET PEOPLE FROM YOUR EARTH KNOW WE'RE ALL REAL.
BUT THEN I FIGURED, DEAN TRIPPE ALREADY KNOWS I'M REAL.
YOU'LL BE SAFE HERE.

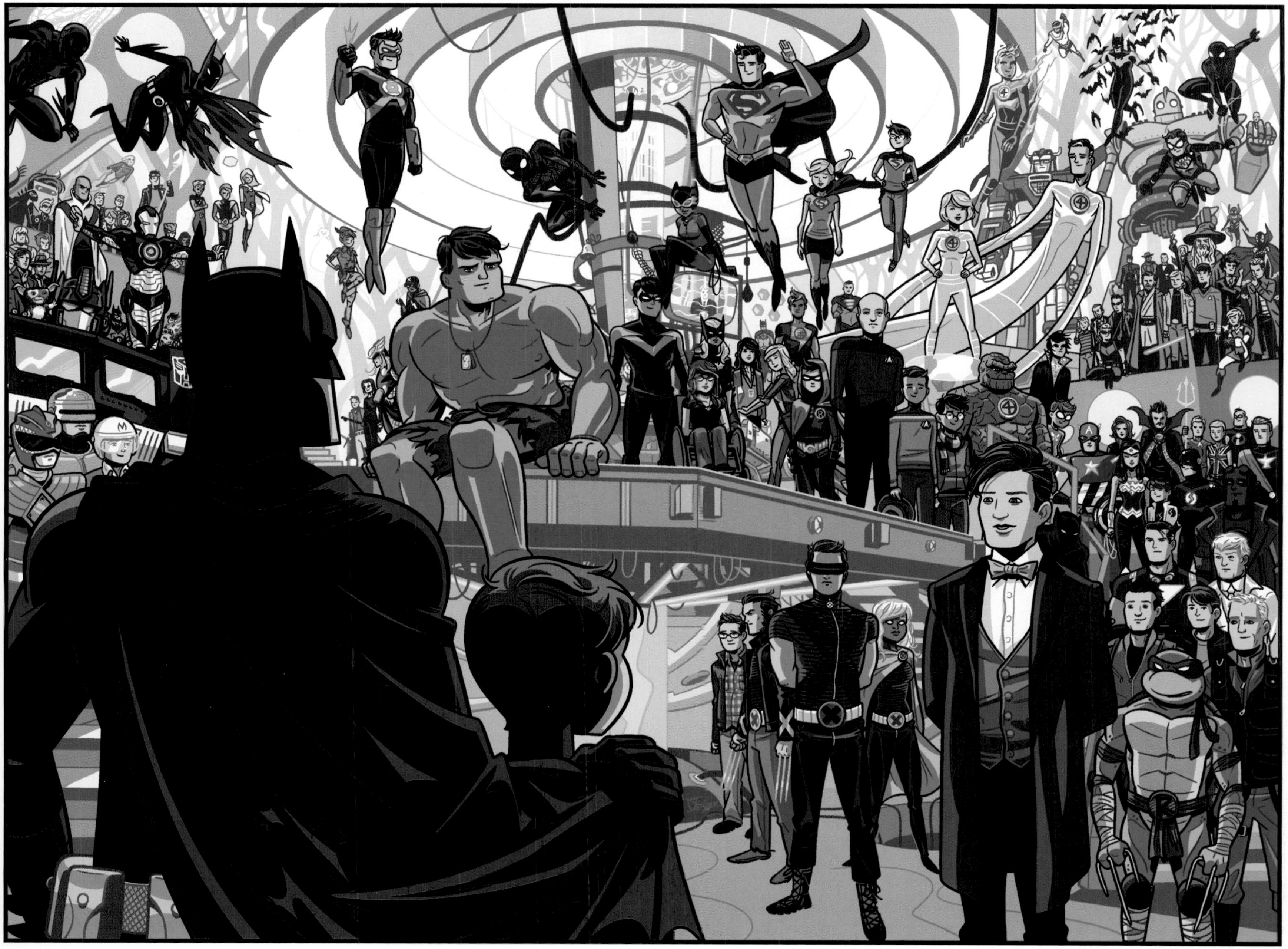

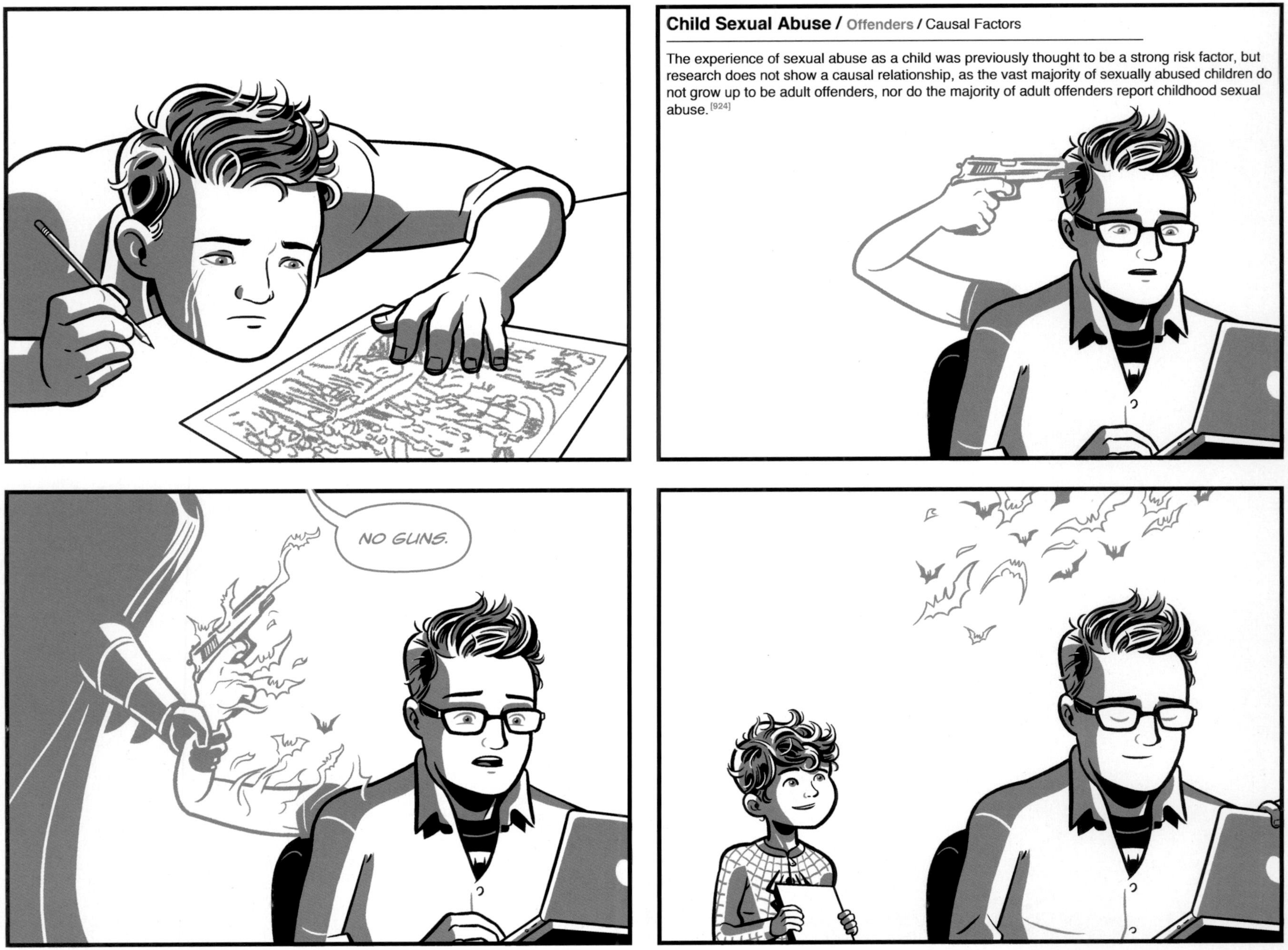
Child Sexual Abuse / Offenders / Causal Factors
The experience of sexual abuse as a child was previously thought to be a strong risk factor, but research does not show a causal relationship, as the vast majority of sexually abused children do not grow up to be adult offenders, nor do the majority of adult offenders report childhood sexual abuse. [924]
NO GUNS.

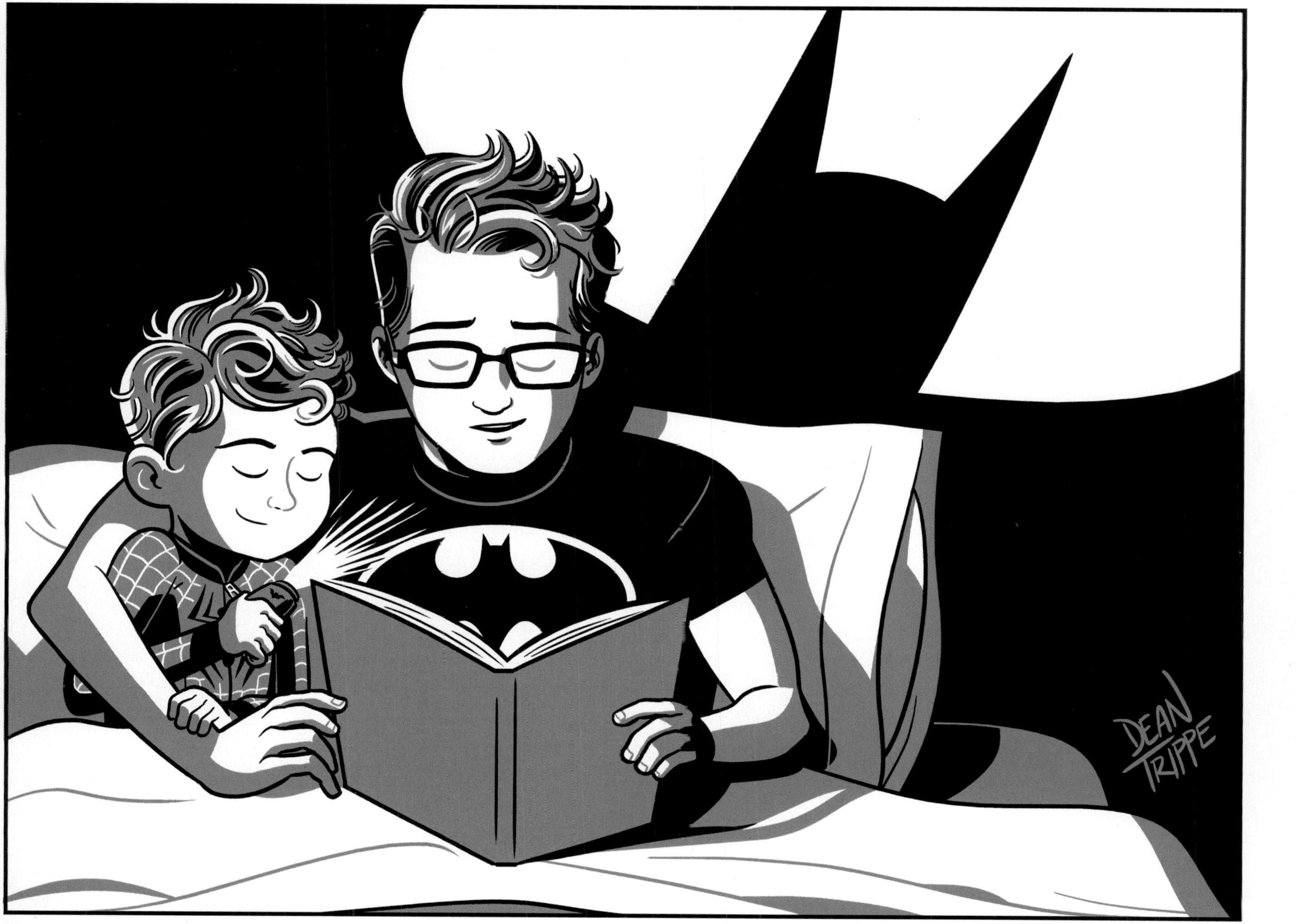
DEAN
TRIPPE

Well, they say to make art for yourself.

I started writing *Something Terrible* a couple of years ago, after a long conversation with a friend, in which I offered my own "secret origin" to explain my deep dislike of psychotic or "broken" depictions of Batman. I told him I felt like Bruce Wayne would've gone crazy if he hadn't become a bat. He needed an outlet for his pain, and had only a child's solution to the unsolvable problem of crime: He became a superhero.

In 1986, my world was broken by two criminals, my biological father, who abandoned his family, like his father had, and a teenager who threatened me with a gun and raped me repeatedly. Luckily for me, and his six other victims, my incredible mom figured out what happened and made sure he was arrested and prosecuted. After the police, the confession, the psychologists, and being assured that my attacker couldn't follow through on his threats, I was sent back to school. It felt like I was in the darkness alone for years, surrounded by peers who hopefully had no idea how terrible people could be. I felt that lonliness until the last week of fifth grade, when the teachers let us watch the 1989 *Batman* movie.

I already liked Batman as much as the next kid, from watching *Super Friends* and the Adam West show, but I'd never seen his origin story. When Michael Keaton flashed back to his childhood trauma, it struck a chord in me I don't think I could've articulated at the time. But I think it was the simple message of all good superhero stories: You are who you choose to be. It's not what happens to you that makes you who you are, but what you choose to do with it. Use all of your abilities to help everyone you can.

I bought my first Batman comic a few weeks later. It's hard to overstate the effect that movie day had on my life. Thanks, Mrs. Bryan.

As I grew older, I became interested in criminal justice, I watched a ton of procedural cop shows. I was especially interested in any episodes that dealt with child molesters, but was horrified to hear, over and over again, that these criminals were apparently just former victims inflicting the crimes of their own attackers upon more innocent victims, like my father had, when he carried on his family's tradition of leaving one's children. I swore to take my own life if I ever had sexual thoughts about children.

My history had made me into someone who had to protect children, even if that meant from myself.

It's horrible, living in fear that there's something terrible inside you, like you might be some secret monster, requiring constant vigilance lest the beast take over. In the 90s, the pervasive "cycle of violence" myth had infected our public consciousness. Nearly every police procedural I've ever seen deal with the subject, to this day, has perpetuated it.

I struggled with my sexuality, at one time believing the idiots who say that being molested somehow makes you gay, despite my attraction to women. On that subject, I want to say that I have never been bullied or made to feel unsafe by my gay friends, unlike straight dudes, who may forever be assessed first as potential threats before I can consider them potential friends.

I lived my whole life wanting to be a father, to finally break the chain of abandonment in my poisoned family tree, but I also lived in fear of having a son, in case I was hopelessly corrupted by my childhood experiences. I prayed for a daughter. Having two awesome sisters predisposed me to thinking that would work out alright. I ended up having the best and brightest son in the world, but I avoided changing diapers or helping with bath time. His mother knew of my history, but I don't think my precautions helped our already doomed relationship.

I drew the first version of the rescue scene in this story a few years ago, after getting over the fear that I might accidentally rewrite time by inviting the heroes of other universes into ours. That's what I get for reading so many Grant Morrison comics. Look, I don't mess with time travel. My son's the best thing to ever happen to me, and I wouldn't change a second of my life, if it meant not having him here. But the day I drew the first pencil sketch of Batman putting his arm around six-year-old me, I was changed. Of course he came to save me. Superheroes don't let bad things happen to kids.

Later that same night, I found myself reading about child sexual abuse on Wikipedia, but was stunned to discover that not only did most victims not become offenders themselves (of course not, the statistics are too horrifyingly high for that to be true), but that most offenders weren't even victims! I was set free. I was finally able to put down the invisible gun I'd diligently kept aimed at my head since I was a child. If you're a survivor of child sexual abuse, I made this comic just to let you know there's not something terrible lurking inside you.

Over the last few years, I found out a lot of things I didn't know about the two crimes that defined my life. I found out that my biological father was alive, with a history of abandoning other families, spending his years in and out of jail. I found out my rapist's name, and that he's repeatedly been incarcerated as well, most recently for driving drunk the wrong way down a median road, with his kid in the car. The worst thing about real monsters is that they don't just slink back into the dark.

I also learned that my mom had started dating my new dad when this happened, and that it was all she could do to keep him from killing the guy. My mom's name is Sarah Trippe, and she's the strongest person I have ever met. My adoptive dad, Charlton Trippe, has always had my back and believed in me. I'm proud to carry his name. The real heroes of my life are my parents. Batman was a good symbol, a good model a kid like me could understand.

I was alone in the darkness. The story of Batman helped me realize that I could wrap it around my arms like a security blanket. Or a cape. I put a yellow oval on my chest, an innocent light now defended by a creature more powerful than anything criminals could throw at me. A creature of the night, something terrible. A bat.

And eventually, I brought Batman to our world in a comic, and somehow it really did change my story.

Thanks for reading it.

Dean Trippe
deantrippe@gmail.com

KICKSTARTER BACKERS

A Comic Shop
A.I. Ruiz
A.J. Howard
A.J. Velasquez
A.K. Pratt
Aaron Brassea
Aaron Haaland
Abby T. Miller
Adam Connor
Adam Daughhetee
Adam Davis
Adam Del Re
Adam Edward Ham
Adam Gunnar Vikström
Adam ILLUS Wallenta
Adam J. Monetta
Adam Lubitow
Adam Mollinger
Adam Platt
Adam Reyes
Addy Schneider
Al Vernacchio
Al-Jania
Alan Jacon
Alan Kistler
Alan Sparrow
Albert Cua
Alberto Rojas Ré
Alberto Thais Parrilla Moruno
Alex
Alex Blair
Alex C.S. Roy
Alex Chung
Alex L.
Alex Reeves
Alex Rudolph
Alex Stinson
Alex Stone
Alex Zalben
Alex de Campi
Alexandra Bell
Alexandra McKenzie
Ali Mattu
Alison Berry
Aliza W.
Allen Campbell
Allen Holt
Allen J. Fuller, III
Alrissa Sia

Alvin Sumigcay
Amanda Clare Lees
Amy Chu
Amy Dittmeier
Amy Lyons
Amy Reeder
Amy-Jayne McGarry-Thickitt
Andi
Andie Luke
Andrea Shockling
Andrew Davis
Andrew Hurley
Andy Haigh
Andy Ihnatko
Andy Lee
Andy Manley
Angela Amiralian
Angela Brett
Angela D. McLaughlin
Angi Shearstone
Angie Mathues
Anie Miles
Anita Nallathamby
Anne Cahalan
Anne Langston
Anne O'Keefe
Antar Ellis
Anthony Hair
Anthony R. Cardno
Arely Diaz
Art Valenzuela
Arthur C. Adams
Arune Singh
Ash Boehnlein
Ash Carskaddon
Ash Harper
Ash Turner
Ashlee Cunningham
Ashley Odenthal
Ashley Raburn
Asia al-Massari
Assaf Vestin
Audrey Vitin
Aurelia & Veronica Montgomery
Autumn N. Johnson
Ballookey Klugeypop
Bannister
Barbara Guttman
Beatrix Ho

Ben Acker
Ben Anderson
Ben Huang
Ben Mitchell
Ben Whitaker
Ben Woo
Bert
Beth Leitman
Biff Mooney
Bill Zanowitz
Blaine
Blair Campbell
Blake Skidmore
Bob Balfour
Bobby Pendarvis
Bobby Timony
Brad Owens
Brandon J. Beane
Brandon Lee
Brandon Lieu
Brandon Vessey
Brandon Viruet
Brandt Dudziak
Brandy Ybarra
Braz Brandt
Bre Edgar
Brett Gordon
Brett White
Brian Doyle
Brian K. Pittman
Brian Loggins
Brian Rose
Brian Stewart
Brian Tatosky
Brianna Dragoo
Brittany Kelley
Brittany Wilbert
Brontis Shane Orengo
Bry Kotyk
Bryan Holmes
Buzzy Buzzlab
C. Skender
C. Storm Bennett
Caitlin Rosberg
Caleb Underwood
Canada Keck
Candace Ming
Cara Gayle Sherman
Carl Moon

Caroline T. Gilroy
Carolyn Livingston
Carolyn Paplham
Caterina Marietti
Catherine Dobbs
Catherine R.L. Lawson
Cecil E. Monkey
Celina L.
Chad Anderson
Chad Maupin
Chad Shipley
Chad Wrataric
Chadwick Torseth
Charlie Kirchoff
Charlotte R. Hollingsworth
Charmaine & Alice Cooke
Chas! Pangburn
Chelsea Craig
Chelsea Swallow
Chendamoni Beaty
Chi Thai
Chris Call
Chris Day
Chris Gentilello
Chris Gladis
Chris Kemple
Chris LeBlanc
Chris Piers
Chris Richardson
Chris Samnee
Chris Shields
Christa L. Jennings
Christal Y.
Christian F.
Christian Smith
Christine Bennett
Christopher Alvarez
Christopher Chettle
Christopher Hooker
Christopher Hull
Christopher Jones
Christopher R. Scotten
Christopher Schiebel
Christopher Ta
Christopher Thomas
Chuck Cottrell
Chuck of WatchaReading.com
Chunk Kelly
Claire Curley Petrillo

Clint Jenkins
Cody Neil
Colette Bennett
Colin Campbell
Colin Cronin
Colin Smith
Consuelo Ruybal
Corinna Vigier
Cortney Webb
Courtney Hartley
Courtney Rose Roberts
Craig Browning
Craig Bryson
Craig Stephen Jones
Craig Welsh
Cristina Lazala
Crystal & Ty Hudson
Crystal Darrisaw
Cullen Bunn
Cully Hamner
Cynthia Ramey
D-Log
DJ Blue Lantern
Dallan Baumgarten
Dan Billings
Dan Bishop
Dan Callahan
Dan Goldman
Dan Hipp
Dan Pollack
Dan Taylor
Dana Rae
Dana Seilhan
Daniel Diehl
Daniel F.
Daniel Govar
Daniel Monson
Daniel Remel
Danny "ShmilS" Appel
Darkshifter
Darren Calvert
Darren LaRose
Darren Rawlings
Dave Caolo
Dave Roman
Dave Stokes
Dave Wheeler
David & Gretchen Hill
David B. Chi

David Bednar	Emily Skahill	Gord Clement	James Tynion, IV	Jessica Russum
David Bishop	Emma Dipple	Gordon McAlpin	James "Rodders" Rodrigues	Jessie Bailey
David Brener	Erech Overaker	Greg Allen	Jamie Jeans	Jesus Enriquez
David Cilley	Eric & Lucy Gignac	Greg Hyatt	Jamie Tanner	Jill Garvin
David Golbitz	Eric Fong	Greg Menzie	Janna Hochberg	Jim Lind
David Harper	Eric Johns	Greg Pak	Janna O'Shea Zagari	Jim McClain
David Harris	Eric Trujillo	Gregory Davis	Jannemieke Hanhart	Jo Price-Murray
David J. Rust	Eric Ways	Guy Thomas	Jaroslaw Ejsymont	Joanne Wong-Toi
David Lucardie	Eric Wight	Hamish Steele	Jasmine P.	Jodie Wood
David Malki !	Eric Wong	Hamster Rage	Jason Best, LCSW	Jody Houser
David Ramsbottom	Erik Burnham	Hannah Warner	Jason D. Allen	Joe Blackwell
David Schwab	Erik Nelson	Harald Stigare	Jason Haddix	Joe D!
Dawn Little	Erika White	Harris Miller	Jason Hernandez	Joe Dunn
Dean Haspiel	Erin Lee Davis	Heart Home Farm	Jason Lapadula	Joe Gillespie
Deborah Poole Gibbs	Erin Riggsmith	Heather Harper	Jason Minor	Joe Glass
Deborah Wallin	Escape Pod Comics	Heather Hogan	Jason R. Harr	Joe Grunenwald
Deena Singer	Estee Kalina	Heather Nygaard	Jason R. Merrill	Joe Karg
Del Hewitt Jr.	Eugenia M. Pinzón Balam	Helder Mira	Jason Roberts	Joel Califa
Derek Buhrke	Evan Schaeffer	Helen Mackness	Jason Rodriguez	Joel Carroll
Derek E. Villanueva	Evan Slash Peterson	Heng Wee Tan	Jason of Melting Records	Joel Priddy
Derek Groothuis	Evan Tarlton	Henrik Norberg	Jay Ewald	John Antram
Derek Hoffman	Fabian Ojeda	Heroes & Fantasies	Jay Faerber	John Bedovian
Derek Mantle	Fantom Comics	Hillarie Gowers	Jay Perry	John Bintz
Derrick Penny	Felipe Sobreiro	HobbitFromPA	Jayme Watson	John Broglia
Diana M. Rodriguez	Fernando Del Bosque	Holden Leung	Jean Robison	John Dailey
Diana Mallery	Fidel Romero	Holly E. Holt	Jeanita Cantrell	John Deemer
Diana Terrill Clark	Finn Neuik	Hyeondo Park	Jeanna Iammarino	John Fennimore
Diane Bonasso	Fionn Ó Maoileoin	Ian & Nicole Mattingly	Jeff Allen	John Hergenroeder
Dirk Manning	For Meridith, from Scott	Ignacio Alcuri	Jeff Martens	John Holmes
Don Cima	Francisco Aranda	Ivan Sivak	Jeff Ray	John Holttum
Don The Idea Guy	Franck Martin	Ivy B. Gladstone	Jeff Reid	John Larison
Donna N. Blitzen	Frankie Escalante	Izzy Mar	Jeff Troutman	John Marcotte
Donne Masaki	Fred & Andrea Clayton	J. Robert Deans	Jeff Wade	John Payne
Doreen Reinbacher	Fred Chamberlain	J.D. Boucher	Jeffrey Chaves	John Sitton
Dorothy P.	Fredrick Thomas	J.G. Colombe	Jen McKernan	John Wimmer
Dr. Billy Carver	G.K. Masterson	J.G. Morales Villanueva	Jenn Skinner	Jon Morris
Dr. David Jabs	Gabe "MightyNightOwl" Arellano	Jack Cole	Jenn Trippe	Jon Scrivens
Drew Robbins	Gabriel Lee	Jack LW Chambers	Jenna Andersen	Jonah Berk
Drew Tabb	Gail Brosnan	Jack Reneau	Jennifer G.	Jonathan Chiaravalle
Duane Murray	GameMastersComic.com	Jaclyn Harmeyer	Jennifer Joseph	Jonathan Edward Goodman
Dustin Drase	Gary Tyrell	Jacob Pauli	Jeremy Disbrow	Jonathan Lareva
E.J. LeBlanc	Gavin Moore	Jad Cooksey	Jerry Douglas	Jonathan Petersen
Ed Peterson	Geek Crash Course	Jake Life	Jerzy Drozd	Jonathan Smith
Edward Wellman	George A. Tramountanas	James C. Tompson	Jesse Mejia	Jonathan Walters
Egg Embry	George Mowry	James Fowler	Jessi Sheron	Jonny Rice
Elaine Ou	Gerry Cardinal III	James Fox Corpuz	Jessibels	Jordan Gibson
Elias Bardas	Gia Hy Dang	James Hsiao	Jessica Beasley	Joseph Gray
Elisabeth Clendenin	Ginny Milling	James Maslowski	Jessica Eleri Jones	Joseph Lockridge
Elizabeth-Amber Love	Glynis Mitchell	James Riley	Jessica McIlveen	Joseph Nguyen

Joseph Patrick O'Connell
Josh Coffey
Josh Elder
Josh Gorfain
Josh Marowitz
Josh Rain
Joshua Yehl
Josué Cardona
José Luis Gutiérrez Valdez
Jude Deluca
Julia Bodura
June St. James
Justin Allen
Justin Andrew Hoke
Justin Beard
Justin Gray
Justin Life
Justin Newberry
Justin Rich
Justin Warren
Justus Hepburn
Jorgen Pedersen
K & N Gibbons
K. Amey
K. Jeffery Petersen
K.F. Dimopoulos
Kaebel JK Hashitani
Kara & Matt Austin
Karen Green
Kari Collins
Karissa Durler
Karl Savage
Kashif Cheema
Kat Greene
Kate Haskell
Kate Moon
Kate Tripoli
Katherine S.
Kathryn Marusik
Katie Guffey
Katie Lopez
Katie Morrow
Katie Stephens
Katie Wheeler
Katrina Goodwin
Katrina Lehto
Katt Tewksbury
Keith Lloyd
Kelly Cassidy

Kelly Thompson
Kelsey Rowe
Ken Borbon
Kenneth Chin
Kenneth Mulrooney
Kenny Kuchnir
Kevin Blankenship
Kevin Edward Walker
Kevin Hand
Kevin Malgesini
Kevin Metz
Kevin Tian
Kevin Volo
Kevin van Haaren
Kier Duros
Kieron Gillen
Kikki Guinn
Kim Belair
Kim Wilgus
Kimberly & Nakeeya
Kimberly M. Cooper
Kit Waddingham
Kjerstin G.
Kohl Glass
Kris Pradipta
Kris Straub
Kristafer Anka
Kristen King
Kristin Hackett
Kristina Collins
Kristy Westaway
Kurt Belcher
Kurt Busiek
Kyle & Emma Jones-Phillipson
Kyle Cooper
Kyle Grant Augustine
Kyle W. Faucher
L. Jamal Walton
L.M. Smith
Lacie Marie Laurendine
Lara Taylor
Larisa Allen & David Zubkoff
Larry Gross
Larry McAllister, II
Laura & Alex Briggs
Laura & Randy Martin
Laura Daigle
Laura Given
Laura Gjovaag

Laura Indick
Laura Johnson
Laura Taylor
Laura von Starschedel Foutz
Lauren
Lauren Amendola
Lauren Ashley Scott
Lauren Gee Myers
Laurent Lehmann
Lee Post
Les McClaine
Liam Dinneen
Lije Carpenter
Lily Ball
Lily Ye
Linda Takahashi
Lindsay L. Olvera
Liz Baughman
Lorena Woodfine
Lorin Killgrove
Lorinda Adams
Lou Lopez
Lyn Cullen
Lyvia A. Martinez
M. Macropoulos
M. Sweeney Lawless
M.A. Solko
Maggie Peavler
Mandy Wultsch
Manuel Caban
Mapet
Marc Casilli
Marc Riemer
Marc Steinijans
Marcel Janse van Vuuren
Marco V. Gutierrez
Margaret Rojahn
Maria Ey. Luihn
Maria Godebska
Maria Sandmo
Marian De Kleermaeker
Mariel Concepcion
Mario Candelaria
Marios Poulimenos
Mark Boettcher, M.D.
Mark Cleary
Mark Morris
Martin Jones
Martin O'Connor

Martin Tapalla
Martin Wendel
Marty Mulkey, LMFT
Masayuki Hashimoto
Mathew Quitney
Mathieu Doublet
Mathilde Tamae-Bouhon
Matie Argiropoulos
Matt Bayne
Matt Gray
Matt Knowles
Matt Pierce
Matt Powers
Matthew J. Hernandez
Matthew Lennon
Matthew Middleton
Matthew O'Deegan
Matthias Kraft
Meg Elliot
Meghan A. Murphy
Melanie C. Duncan
Melanie Carson
Melanie Stapel
Melissa Hannum
Melissa Kay
Melissa Railey
Melissa Trender
Menachem Luchins
Meredith Lock
Michael Bohli
Michael C. Fedoris
Michael Cravens
Michael Farah
Michael Geaney
Michael Hoffert Jr.
Michael Howard
Michael J. Ahlers
Michael Nixon & Diana Dekajlo
Michael Stevens
Micheal Ada
Michele
Michelle Blum
Michelle Cerullo
Michelle Manning
Michelle "rawretzrobin" Tan
Mighty J.M. Hunter
Mikael Martinez
Mike Aragona
Mike Exner, III

Mike Fatum
Mike Greear
Mike Mitchell
Mike Norton
Mike Oestreicher
Mike Okeke
Mike Roe
Mike Weldon
Ming Doyle
Ming Han Sidney Reuben Lim
Ming Siu Goh
Miniyuna
Miriam Busch
Mohammed N.
Molly B.
Molly Cady
Molly McBride
Nancy & Danny Wilson
Nancy Leah Williams
Natalie Abinante
Nate Anderson
Nate Itzen
Nathan Plank
Nathan Schulz
Nathan Seabolt
Nathan Wainwright
Nathaniel Booth
Nic29
Nicholas Zamora
Nick Davis
Nick Elias
Nick Hines
Nick Spencer
Nicolas Barrière-Kucharski
Nikki Frankel
Nirakone Phromkharanourak
Nixie
Nny Witham
Noah & Eli Spencer
Nuha Jalal
Olivera Teodorovic
Olotie
Ora Peng
OsbournDraw
Oscar "Ask" Wiberg
Owen Choules
PSJ
Pablo Arriaga
Pat Quinn

Patricia Lupien
Patrick O'Connor
Patrick Rennie
Patrick Tran
Patrick West
Patrick Y. Lagua
Patrik Ulander
Paul @DjNawtso Quick
Paul Milligan
Paul Owen McDonald
Paul R. Schwarber
Paulo Eugênio
Peggy Delaney
Phil Hester
Phill Warren
Páll Brim Joensen
Qaantar
R. Manon Skaggs
R.J. Gabriel
Rachael Moody
Rachel A. Cobb
Rachel Dukes
Rachel Edidin & Miles Stokes
Rachel Kozlowski
Ramonesome
Randy Lander
Randy Wood
Rashid "MrWolfbite" Al Kaabi
Raymond Woolcott
Rebecca A. Paisley
Rebecca Camp
Rebecca Nelson
Reesa Herberth
Regina G.
Renard Mccrary Ortiz
Rene Hernandez
Rene Poyyayil
Reza Ali Malik
Richard Gaddy
Richard Vu
Ricky Salinas
Riot Scene! Media
Rob Blakely
Rob Kelly
Rob McDowell
Rob Pugh
Rob Stenzinger
Robert Ahn
Robert Brown

Robert Coles
Robert E. Stutts
Robert Gilson
Robert Johnson
Robert Lawrence
Robert Simpson
Robin Brenner
Rock Shop Music and Comics
Rodney C. Roberts
Rodney Romasanta
Rolando Garcia
Ronnie Mays, Jr.
Rosalia Millan
Rose Miner
Ross Demma
Roy Blumenthal
Ryan Alexander
Ryan Brunsvold
Ryan Cook
Ryan Gray
Ryan Moreau
R~
S. Suzuki
S.F. Konkin
Sam Einhorn
Sam Ellis
Sam Orchard
Sam Razo
Samantha Crane
Samantha Cross
Sambo Virak Touch
Samuel York
Sandy Macdonald
Sara Katherine Horn
Sara Nalley
Sarah & Charlton Trippe
Sarah Baum
Sarah Brick
Sarah Elliot
Sarah Hiraki
Sarah Louise Green
Scott
Scott Beveridge
Scott Carelli
Scott Fogg
Scott M. Hallett
Scott McClellan
Scott Simons
Sean Dove

Sean Liu
Sean M.P. Kennedy
Sean McKeever
Sean S. Yang
Sergio A. Meza
Seth Rosenblatt
Seung Lee
Shakti Lemaris
Shana Carter
Shane Clark
Shane Duffy
Shane Patrick Boyle
Shannon Boepple
Shannon Finch
Shannon McMaster
Shannon Slayton
Shaun Manning
Shay Brog
Sheilah Villari
Shilpa Bhatia
Shilpa Mohite
ShockingPause & Skullea
Sketkh Williams
Sola Adeonigbagbe
Sophy Qualman
Sophya Vidal
Stacey Gonillo
Stacy Poor
Stefan Blitz
Stephanie Luibel Becker
Stephen "Switt!" Wittmaak
Stephen Beaumont
Stephen Couch
Stephen Reid
Stephenie House
Stergios Botzakis
Steve Albertelli
Steve Flack
Steve Jones
Steve McFarland
Steve Pause
Steven Howearth
Steven M. Miller
Steven Mathews
Stu Rase
Subspace Comics
Suri
Susan Fox
Susan Meyer

Susan Renee Page
Susy Cisneros
Sven Müller & Sylvia Nolte
Svend Anderson
Svend Mathiesen, II
Sybil Allaire
T. Perran Mitchell
Tag Murphy
Tamara Brooks
Tasha Gray
Taylor MacSween
Team OJ
Ted Alexander
TeeKetch
Terence, Clare, & Aeryn Chua
Terry Grant
Than Gibson
The Battram-Gregory Family
The Beguiling Books & Art
The Boaz Family
The Kearny Family
The Limbach Family
The Planck Family
The Tharan Family
The Wurtsmith Family
Third Coast Comics
Thom Allard
Thomas Fuchs
Thomas Gagnon
Tim Bond
Tim Daniel
Tim Hodge
Tim Hulsizer
Tim Leong
Tim Meakins
Tim Reynolds
Timmy Vatterott
Timothy Dalton
Timothy R.
Tina MacKinnon
Todd Eckel
Todd Sokolove
Todd Wagner
Tom & Donna Rigsby
Tom Brazelton
Tom Haeussler
Tom Harley
Tom Kelso

Tom Rankin
Tommy Lee Edwards
Tommy Valdez
Travis Ellisor
Travis L. Tidmore, Esq.
Trever H.
Ty Buttars
Unknown Kulture
Vanessa Sjogren
Vaula Rinne
Vi Bergquist
Victoria Sauter
Vince Bayless
Vincent Fung
Vincent Iadevaia
Vincent Justin Mitra
Virginia E. Mead
Vito Delsante
Vixy
Walt Parrish
Warrick Lehmann
Wayne Rée
Wei X
Whit Leopard
Whitley Corrin
Whitney B.
Whitney Drake
Wilder Nutting-Heath
Will J.
William Goodman
William Michels
Wolfgang Lange
Yasmin Liang
Youri Zoutman
Zach Brown
Zach Cole
Zachary Clemente
Zainah Alrujaib
Zuluf Yakingun
grumpyhawk
jerkfish2
not!Player 1
thenumeraltwo
@conmantherad

THANK YOU.

SPECIAL THANKS

Thanks to Bill Finger, long since passed and still uncredited for his vital contributions to building the Batman, the hero who taught me that even a child broken by tragedy and trauma could rebuild himself into someone useful to others. You wrote a fictional story and saved my real life half a century later. That's magic. Thank you.

Immense thanks to Paul Dini and Bruce Timm, for the DC Animated Universe, domain of the Batmanest Batman ever Batman'd. Those versions of the characters were so perfect, I still hear their voices when reading.

Thanks, of course, to Chuck Dixon, for his stewardship of the Bat-Family, especially my fictional bat-brothers and sisters, Dick Grayson, Tim Drake, Barbara Gordon, and Stephanie Brown, and for writing the very first comic book I ever read, Detective Comics #645.

And unending thanks from the start of our hologram universe to the furthest reaches of Hypertime to Grant Morrison, for "I know your secret," for the 853rd Century, for the best Dynamic Duo since the first, for fixing the broken toys, for the machine designed to build a Batman, for the First Truth, and for making me think the superheroes might really save me if I believed in them.

And for real friends and family, thanks to my mom and dad, to my awesome sisters, Jenn and Melody, to my best pals, Jason Horn, Scott Fogg, Ben Acker, Fred Clayton, Dan Remel, Dylan Hansen, Bob Kieffer, Tyler Burnett, and Patrick Rooks, to the love of my life, Candace O'Neal, and to my son, Emmett, who is my light in the sky.

LAST THOUGHTS

When I first published this story online, I figured it would connect with a small overlap of child sexual abuse survivors who also liked superheroes. I grew up in a small town, where I was the only kid in my class who read comics regularly. I guess I didn't fully understand how dramatically the culture had changed, with the rise of popular nerddom and modern superhero media domination. Even knowing the stats of victims like myself, I never expected this.

Something Terrible has now been read by about two million people. It was featured on Huffington Post, The A.V. Club, Upworthy, and nearly every comics news site. I was invited to speak at Comicon International, in a panel about the worst thing that ever happened to me, and how superheroes helped me recover. I knew this book would be the most important thing I'd ever do in comics, but I didn't expect any of this.

The world is big and bad, and as a survivor of something terrible myself, it's often tough to navigate. There are new cases of horrors I'd never even imagined floating through the news feeds every single day. Even comedy shows still treat these crimes as silly in the abstract, a cheap, ever-ready go-to for giggles.

Before Something Terrible, I'd never experienced "triggers," but having reframed my secret origin into a not-so-secret one, I have felt exposed and disconnected daily. I'm humbled to know how many people desperately needed my story, and most of the time, I don't regret it. But if I'm being honest, it's hard. Even revisiting all of this in order to complete this print edition has been tough. I thought doing the digital edition was all the therapy I needed, but I've learned that it's an everyday thing. Always healing. Always training. Just like Batman.

Thank you to everyone who has found me at a convention or written me to express your gratitude or share your story with me. I'll always be there for you, if you need me.

Thank you to everyone who supported this book, not just for themselves, but for all of our bat-brothers and bat-sisters who needed it, too.

In the last year and a half, I've moved into a new home, asked the love of my life to marry me, brought two incredible step-kids into my life, helped launch a truly special comics and games shop, and worked with some of my best friends and heroes in the comics industry. It's been a great year, but also a hard one, with unforeseen setbacks and tests of character. But I'm more hopeful about the future than I've ever been, with new projects on the horizon and new challenges ahead.

I want everyone who reads this book to know that those of us who have faced the darkness in the world aren't infected by it. Knowing there are monsters doesn't make you one. Keep fighting. You've got friends you don't even know yet, just waiting to have your back. If you need to share your story to better process it, do it. If you don't feel that, don't worry about it. You know who you chose to be. That's enough.

Thanks for believing in this project. Now put it in the hands of a friend who needs it. The signal is up. Let's go, Bat-Family.

Dean Trippe
deantrippe.com

EPILOGUE

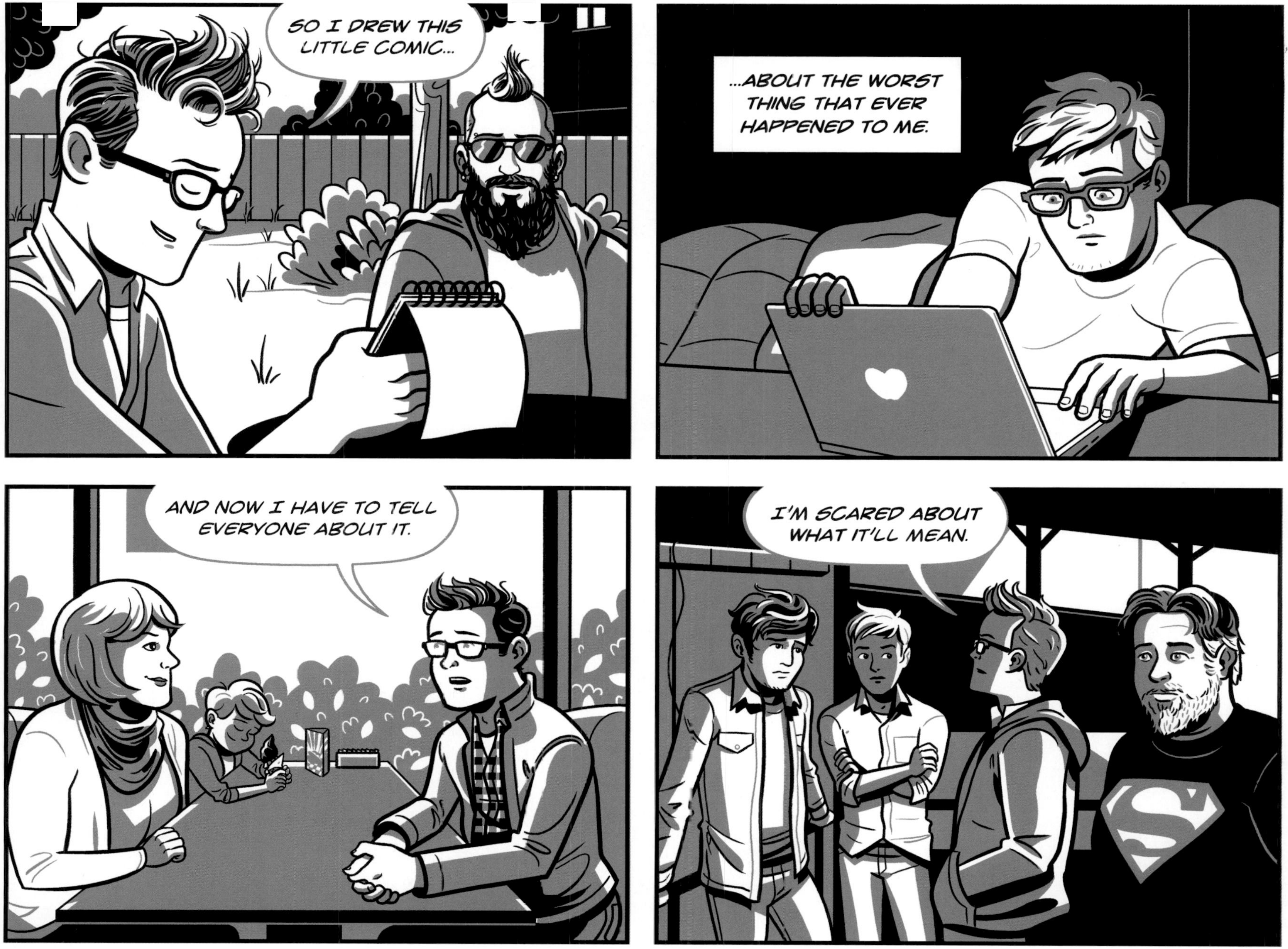
SO I DREW THIS LITTLE COMIC...
...ABOUT THE WORST THING THAT EVER HAPPENED TO ME.
AND NOW I HAVE TO TELL EVERYONE ABOUT IT.
I'M SCARED ABOUT WHAT IT'LL MEAN.

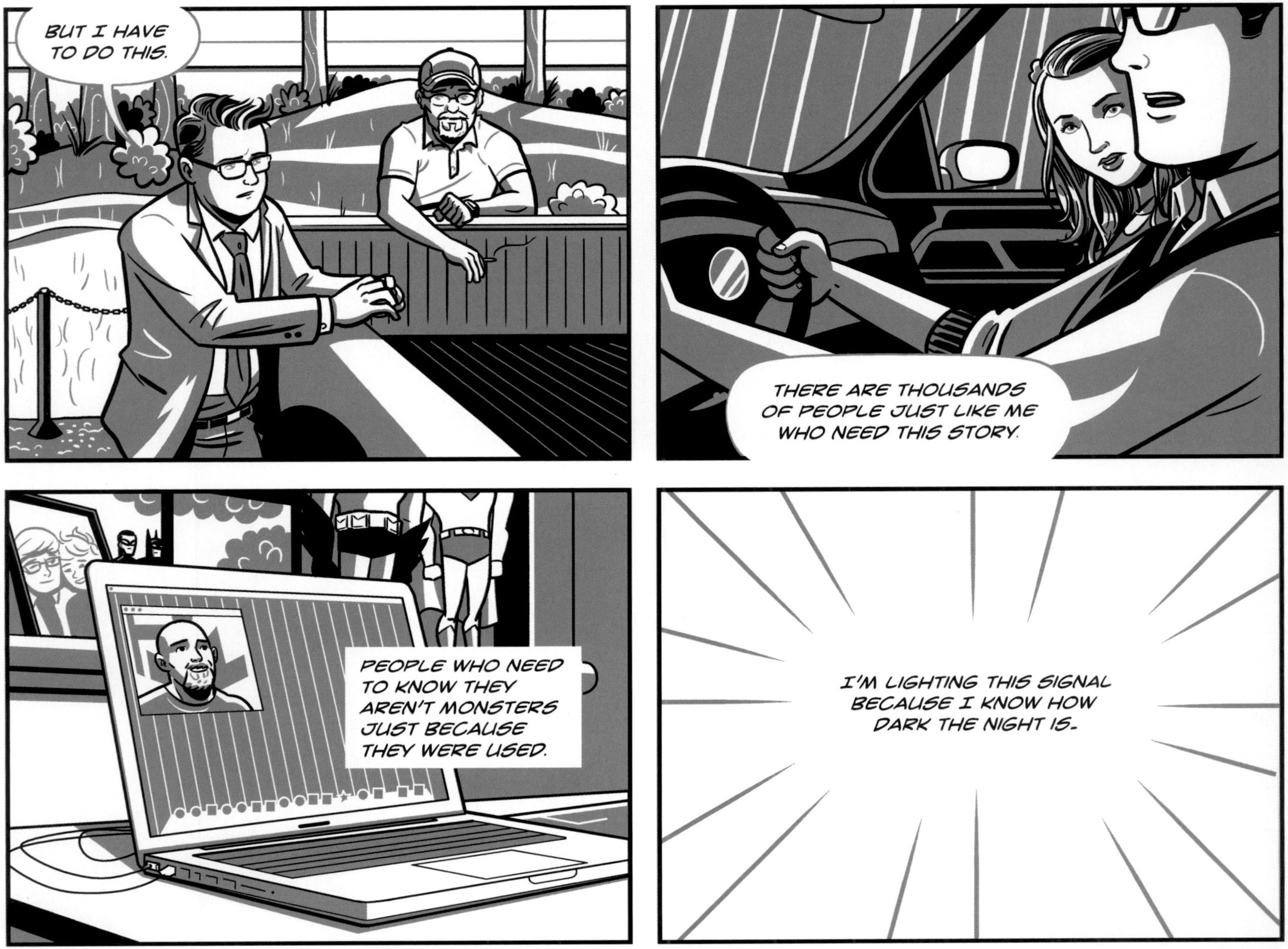
BUT I HAVE TO DO THIS.
THERE ARE THOUSANDS OF PEOPLE JUST LIKE ME WHO NEED THIS STORY.
PEOPLE WHO NEED TO KNOW THEY AREN'T MONSTERS JUST BECAUSE THEY WERE USED.
I'M LIGHTING THIS SIGNAL BECAUSE I KNOW HOW DARK THE NIGHT IS.

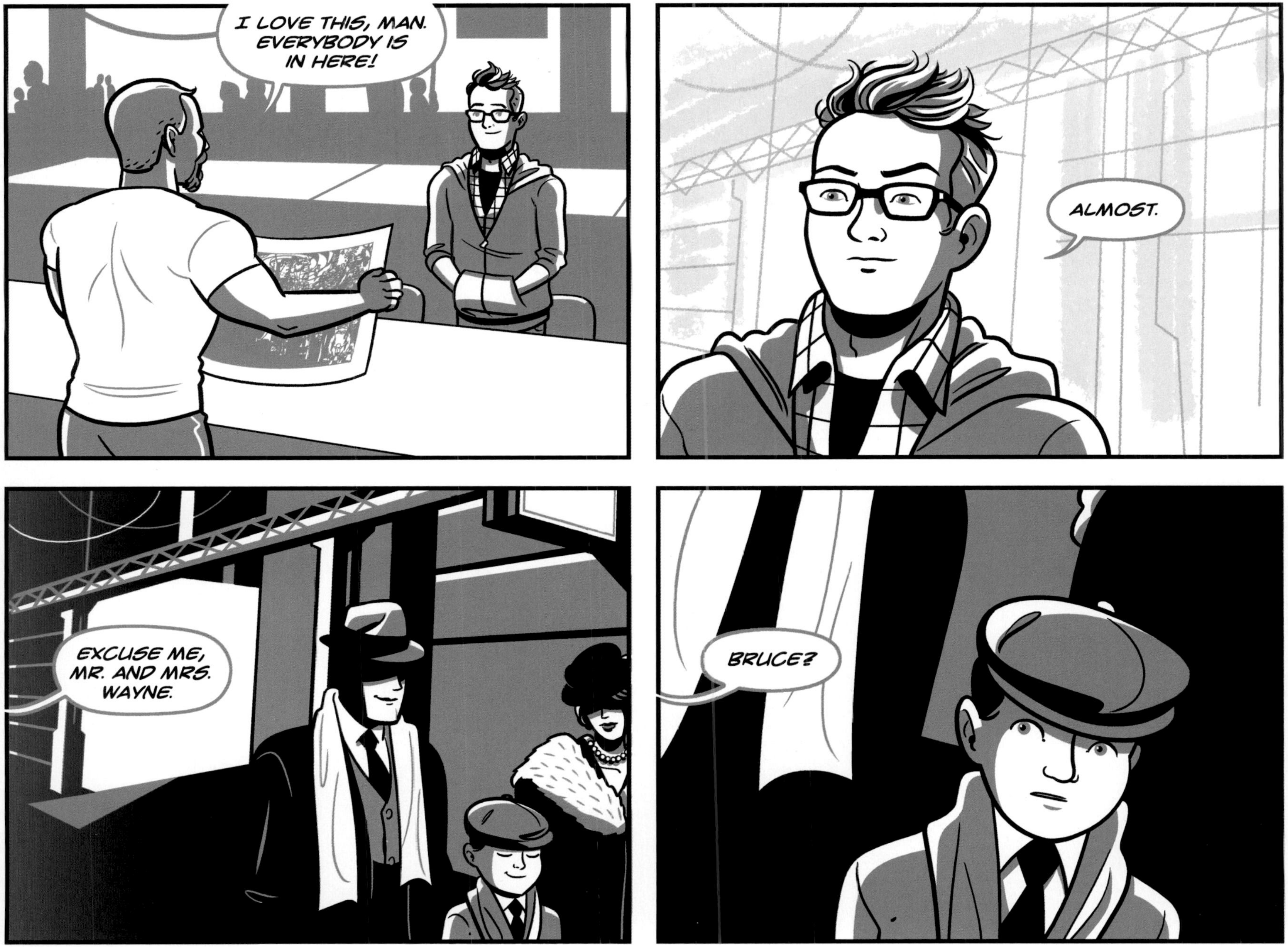
I LOVE THIS, MAN. EVERYBODY IS IN HERE!
ALMOST.
EXCUSE ME, MR. AND MRS. WAYNE.
BRUCE?

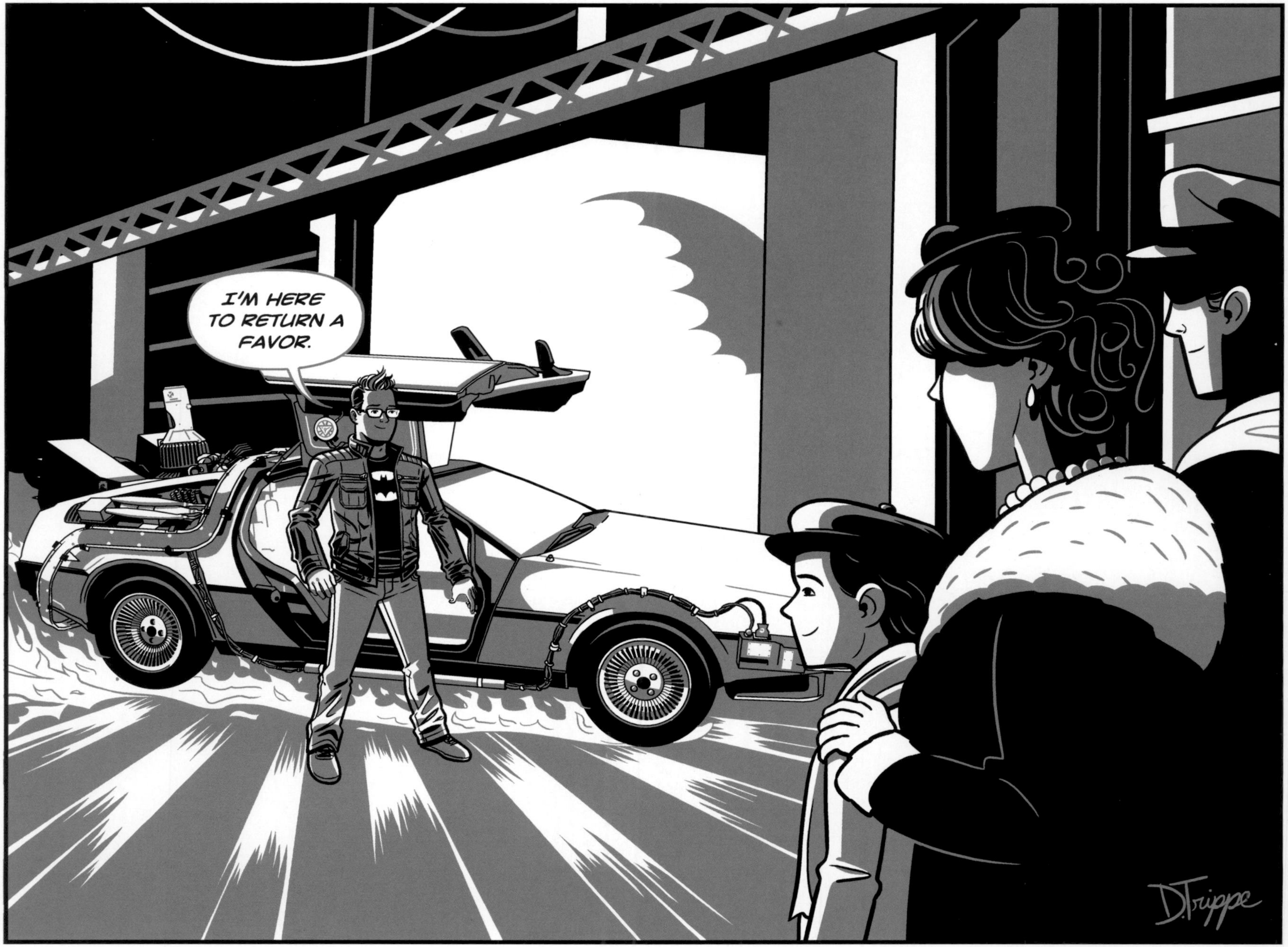
I'M HERE TO RETURN A FAVOR.
D.Trippe

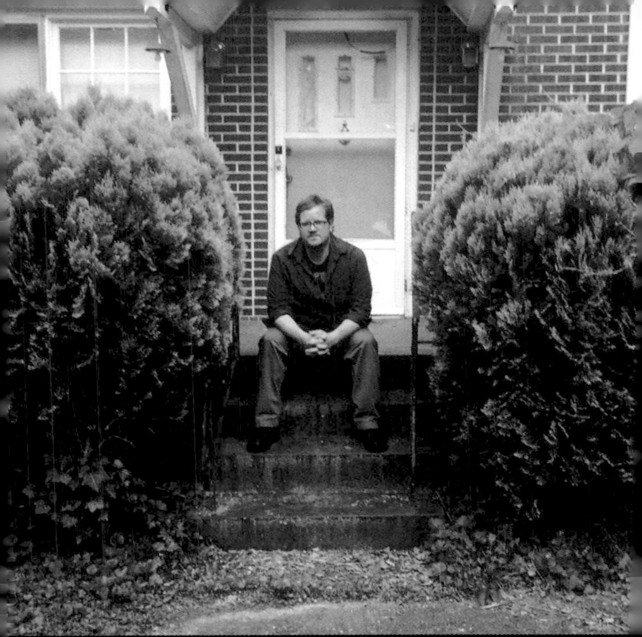

Dean Trippe is the creator of the superhero parody web-comic, *Butterfly*, co-founder and editor of the superhero redesign art site, *Project: Rooftop,* illustrator of Oni Press's *Power Lunch* children's books, and was a contributor to the Eisner and Harvey award-winning anthology, *Comic Book Tattoo.* He is a father, a comic shop manager, a lifelong fan of superheroes, and has an actual degree in comic books.

For more of Dean's work, visit **deantrippe.com**

published by Iron Circus Comics • ironcircus@gmail.com • www.ironcircus.com

Something Terrible © Dean Trippe 2016. All rights reserved. No part of this book may be reprinted or reproduced in any manner (except for journalistic, educational, or review purposes) without written consent of Dean Trippe and Iron Circus Comics. All existing characters copyright their respective owners.

first edition: February 2016 • ISBN: 978-0-9890207-5-6 • printed in China

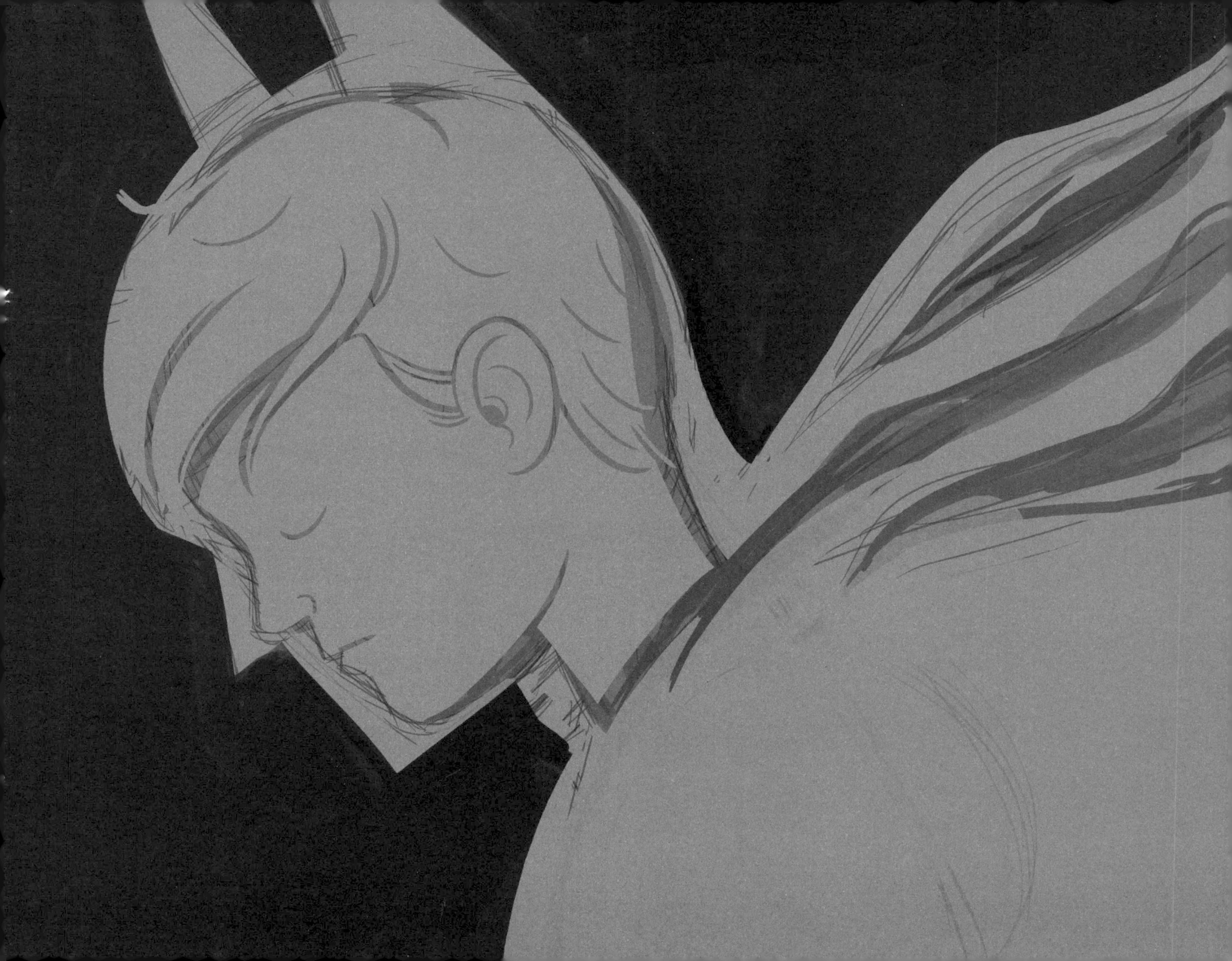